VOLLEYBALL

VOLLEYBALL

MASTERING THE BASICS WITH THE PERSONALIZED SPORTS INSTRUCTION SYSTEM

Jon Poole
Radford University

Michael Metzler
Georgia State University

Allyn and Bacon
Boston   London   Toronto   Sydney   Tokyo   Singapore

VICE PRESIDENT	Paul A. Smith
Publisher	Joseph E. Burns
EDITORIAL ASSISTANTS	Annemarie Kennedy
MARKETING MANAGER	Rick Muhr
EDITORIAL PRODUCTION SERVICE	Bernadine Richey Publishing Services
TEXT DESIGN AND COMPOSITION	Barbara Bert Silbert
MANUFACTURING BUYER	Julie McNeill
COVER ADMINISTRATOR	Brian Gogolin

Internet: www.abacon.com

ISBN: 0-205-32370-7

Printed in the United States of America

10 9 8 7 6 5 4 3 2 1   05 04 03 02 01 00

CONTENTS

PREFACE

INTRODUCTION TO PSIS VOLLEYBALL

Hello, and welcome to your **volleyball class**! That's right, *your* volleyball class. This personal workbook includes almost everything you will need to learn the game of volleyball and become a proficient beginning-level player. Of course, your instructor will play an important part as you progress, but most of what you will need is contained in your Personal Workbook. Your volleyball class will be taught this term using the **Personalized Sports Instruction System (PSIS)**, developed specifically for college basic instruction courses such as the one in which you are enrolled. All of the materials in this workbook have been refined in field tests with many students such as yourself, college men and women getting their first formal volleyball instruction.

The key design feature of the PSIS is that it allows for individualized learning and progression through the course. Think back to other classes you have taken: some students learn faster than others. This is a fact in all learning situations. Depending on individual learning rates, some students become frustrated if the course goes too fast. Others become bored if the course goes too slowly. Either way, many students become disinterested, reducing their enjoyment of the course. For volleyball, the most harmful result of frustration or boredom is that students are not given a proper chance to learn the game and to enjoy it as a regular part of their activity schedule. Whether you are a "bare beginner" or currently have some volleyball experience, the PSIS design will allow you to progress **"as quickly as you can, or as slowly as you need."** Keep this little motto in mind as you become familiar with this workbook and progress through your volleyball class this term.

Another point to keep in mind is that the PSIS is *achievement oriented*. That means the PSIS design is intended to help you learn the necessary skills, strategies, and rules for beginning volleyball play. We guarantee you will be a better player at the end of your PSIS class than you are now!

As you will see, your improvement will come in a way that is different from most other courses you have taken. You will be asked to assume more responsibility for your own learning than ever before. Remember, all the instructional material is included in your Personal Workbook. It will be up to you to learn the contents of the workbook, become familiar with the PSIS system, attend class regularly, follow your instructor's class policies, and work diligently toward completing the course sequences. It has been our experience that college students enjoy taking a large role in their own learning and appreciate the individualized plan of the PSIS. We know that you will, too.

ADVANTAGES OF THE PSIS FOR YOU

1. **The PSIS reduces your dependence on the instructor.** Your Personal Workbook provides nearly all the information you will need to complete the course. All content, learning task, and managerial information is at your fingertips, not with the instructor. When you are ready for a new learning task, the individualized plan will allow you to proceed on your own.
2. **Individualized learning is emphasized.** The PSIS will allow you to learn volleyball "as quickly as you can, or as slowly as you need." You will be able to remain in your own comfort zone while progressing through the course.
3. **You will have increased responsibility for your own learning.** As adult learners, college students can assume responsibility for much of their own learning. You can make decisions that have direct bearing on class attendance, practice routines, and achievement. The PSIS system shifts much of the responsibility and decision making directly to you and away from the instructor.
4. **Your access to the instructor will be increased whenever you need it.** Since PSIS instructors can spend much more time in class teaching students, it means that you will get more personal attention and quality instruction, *that is, if you need it*. If you do not require as much interaction with the instructor, it will not be forced on you as with group learning strategies.
5. **You can chart your own progress.** Your PSIS Volleyball Personal Workbook includes a simple Personal Progress Chart to help you gauge your learning as you go through the course. This will help you to make decisions about your learning pace, projected grade, and how to use your class time most efficiently.

YOUR ROLE IN PSIS VOLLEYBALL

Your role in PSIS Volleyball can be summarized easily: become familiar with and follow the Personal Workbook as an independent learning guide. You will not need to depend on the instructor for content and managerial information. But when the workbook is not sufficient or specific learning information is needed, you should be sure to *ASK FOR HELP*! Your Personal Workbook will provide nearly all the information needed to complete the course. So, if you can progress without the instructor's direction, the system is designed to let you. If you need help, the instructor will be free to provide it for you. Your instructor will show you a *help signal* for getting his or her attention in class. It might be a raised hand or a verbal call. Be sure you know this signal, and do not be shy about using it!

YOUR INSTRUCTOR'S ROLE IN PSIS VOLLEYBALL

Your instructor has the important role of *facilitator* in your PSIS volleyball course. Your Personal Workbook will provide most of the content and management information you will need, providing your instructor more time to give students individual attention. There will be just one large-group demonstration throughout the entire course, and very little time will be spent organizing routine class "chores." Nearly all the instructor's time will be available to facilitate your learning on an individual basis.

Your instructor has the teaching experience and expertise to make the PSIS work as well as it was designed. The PSIS system allows the instructor to provide the maximum use of his or her expertise by *facilitating* the learning process for you.

SKILL AND KNOWLEDGE COURSE MODULES

Your PSIS volleyball course contains a number of learning activities divided into a series of modules. There are two types of modules: **performance skill** and **volleyball knowledge**. Performance skill modules focus on the major psychomotor performance patterns needed to play volleyball. The volleyball knowledge module contains information on basic game rules and volleyball etiquette.

PSIS COURSE MANAGEMENT AND POLICIES

In this section you will learn some of the ways in which the PSIS approach can give you increased control over your own learning. Some course management and policies will come from your Personal Workbook. Others will be communicated to you by your instructor. Be sure that you are familiar with all course management routines and policies.

1. **Dressing for class.** You will need to have proper clothing and footwear in order to participate comfortably and safely in your volleyball class. We suggest that you wear lightweight, loose-fitting clothes that will not restrict your range of motion (shorts, T-shirts, and the like). General-purpose court shoes or "cross training" shoes with white soles are recommended. Do not wear running shoes or shoes that will make marks on the floor. Specialized clothing and volleyball shoes are not necessary. Be sure to ask your instructor about his or her policies regarding dressing for class.

2. **Equipment.** Your instructor will provide you with all the necessary equipment for class, and with the routines for distributing and collecting equipment each day.

3. **Depositing and distributing Personal Workbooks.** Your instructor will advise you on his or her policy regarding your workbook each day after class. We suggest that the instructor collect all student workbooks at the end of class and bring them to class the next day. Be sure that you know the exact policy to be used, since you cannot participate fully in class without your own workbook.

4. **Practice partners.** Some learning tasks will call for you to practice with one or more partners and be checked off by them. Any classmate can be your partner for most tasks. A few tasks will specify that all students in a drill be at the same place in the course learning sequence.

5. **Arriving to class.** Your instructor will inform you about specific routines for arriving to class and beginning each day. Generally, you should (1) arrive at or before the class starting time, (2) locate your own Personal Workbook, (3) complete your stretching and warm-up routine, (4) find a practice partner (if needed at that time), and (5) begin to practice the appropriate learning task. Note that you can begin as soon as you arrive. Except for the first day of instruction, the instructor will not wait to begin the class with all students together. Arriving before class will allow you extra time to practice your volleyball skills.

6. **Self-checks, partner-checks, and instructor-checks.** Each learning task in PSIS volleyball requires that your mastery be documented (checked off). Some tasks can be checked off by you, some must be checked off by a partner, and some by your instructor. Items are checked off by the appropriate person initialing and dating the designated area after each

checked task in your Personal Workbook. Instructor-checked tasks will require that you practice for a period of time prior to attempting mastery and being checked off. When you are ready, indicated by a series of successful trial blocks, signal the instructor and ask him or her to observe you. If you do not reach the stated criterion, you can return for more practice and signal again for the instructor at a later time. *There is no penalty for not making a mastery criterion. You can try as many times as it takes to be successful.* You may find it helpful to alert the instructor at the beginning of a class in which you anticipate needing his or her observation and checking. The instructor will then be on the lookout for your signal.

7. **Grading.** Your course instructor will inform you about the grading system and related policies to be used in your PSIS volleyball class. Be sure you are aware of the specific requirements and procedures for determining your grade.

USING YOUR TIME EFFECTIVELY

Your PSIS volleyball course is made up of a series of predetermined learning tasks grouped into seven modules. Your course will have a set number of class days with a set class length. It is important for you to know your own learning pace and to make steady progress toward completing all course requirements. Therefore, you will need to learn how to best use your time in class and to accurately project completion of PSIS volleyball before the end of the term. Here are some helpful tips for managing your time.

1. Arrive to class early and begin right away. No signal will be given by the instructor for class to begin.
2. Stay for the entire class period. Do not get into a habit of leaving early.
3. Learn the PSIS course management system right away. The quicker you understand how it works, the sooner you can start using it to your advantage.
4. Do not hesitate to ask the instructor for assistance. Learn and use the class help signal to get the instructor's attention.
5. If there is not enough time to complete a new task in a class, at least *start* it. This will save time the next day.
6. When you are close to finishing a task at the end of a class, try to stay a few minutes late to complete it. This avoids repetitious setup time the next day and the possible loss of your learning momentum.
7. When a practice partner is needed, pair up with the first person you can find, rather than waiting for a certain person. (This is good way to get to know more of your classmates!)
8. Alert the instructor prior to instructor-checked criterion tasks so that he or she will be available when you need observation and a check-off.

PSIS VOLLEYBALL LEARNING MODULES

This section will describe how the PSIS course learning modules are designed. It is important that you know how the PSIS works so that you can take advantage of its individualized learning features. The course learning content is included in two kinds of learning modules: **performance skill** and **volleyball knowledge**.

Each *performance skill* module will include the following:

1. A written **introduction** to the skill
2. An **instructor demonstration** of the proper skill techniques
3. Text and photographs that explain the **components** or **phases** of each skill
4. Photographs that highlight the key **performance cues** (these same cues will be presented by the instructor in his or her demonstration).
5. Simple **comprehension tasks** and **readiness drills** to develop initial skill patterns
6. An **error analysis** and **correction section** for self-analyzing common mistakes
7. **Learning tips** for increased proficiency
8. A series of several **criterion tasks** for practicing and demonstrating your skill mastery
9. One or more **challenge tasks** for developing tactical applications of skills in modified competitive situations
10. A **Personal Recording Form** for selected tasks, used to record successful practice trials

The *volleyball knowledge* module will include:

1. A **reading** on the basic rules of volleyball and volleyball game strategy
2. A **knowledge quiz** to test your understanding of the rules and strategy

CHARTING YOUR PROGRESS

The last page of your PSIS volleyball workbook includes your **Personal Progress Chart**. Your instructor will show you how to correctly label the chart, and the rest is very simple. At the end of each week in the course, put an x above that date, and across from the last task you completed. As the weeks go by, you will begin to see how your individual learning pace projects your successful completion of all course learning modules.

This introductory section, combined with additional information from your instructor, will allow you to use the PSIS volleyball workbook to your full advantage and to learn volleyball at your own pace, with highly individualized attention from your instructor. Because PSIS volleyball is a complete system for learning the game, it might take you a little time to become familiar with this approach. However, remember that your instructor is there to help when you have questions about the system and when you need individual attention for learning. Now that you know about the PSIS volleyball system, you are probably anxious to get started. We hope you enjoy learning volleyball with the PSIS approach and that you will become an avid player of this lifelong game. READY...SET...GO!!

MODULE **1**

STARTING OUT RIGHT
STRETCHING FOR VOLLEYBALL

INTRODUCTION

Flexibility refers to the ability of the muscles, tendons, and ligaments around a joint to move, while providing support and allowing the joint to move smoothly through its entire range of motion. Increased flexibility means more supple muscles, which reduces the risk of injury to the muscle when the limb is moved suddenly. The static method is the most commonly recommended stretching technique. It has been shown to be extremely effective in increasing the range of motion and, when done slowly and carefully, presents little chance of injury to the muscles.

Some sports and forms of exercise lead to improved flexibility of the involved body part. Volleyball, for example, tends to limber the shoulder joint and lower back. Gymnastics can only be accomplished with a high degree of flexibility in virtually all points of the body. Activities such as walking and jogging do not require a large range of motion and do not increase flexibility. This is why it is important that stretching should precede these types of exercises. Stretching not only enhances performance, but also reduces the risk of injury.

Flexibility should be included during the warm-up phase of an exercise program. This allows for gentle stretching of muscles around the joint before vigorous movement and leads to a slower cool-down, thereby maintaining local blood flow and reducing postexercise soreness. Although muscular soreness can have many origins, one major cause appears to be damage to the connective tissue elements in the muscles and tendons. No one method of overcoming soreness is available, but adequate stretching appears to aid not only in preventing soreness, but also in relieving it when it already exists.

PERFORMANCE CUES

1. **Warm-up.** Protect the muscle by beginning with a low- to moderate-intensity warm-up for 2 to 3 minutes prior to performing strenuous stretching exercises. Running in place should provide an excellent warm-up.

2. **Do not bounce.** Move into the stretching position slowly, continuing until mild tension is felt. Utilize a static or very slow stretch and hold the position. A ballistic or bouncing stretch can be counterproductive and even cause injury.

3. **Hold the stretch.** The stretch position should be held for a predetermined amount of time. It is suggested that the initial holding position be between 15 and 20 seconds and be gradually increased over the following weeks. As flexibility improves, attempt to hold the stretch slightly longer. When the stretching exercise is complete, the body should be released slowly from the stretch position.

4. **Target Zone.** You should not feel pain when stretching a muscle. There is a stretching target zone where *there is tension in the muscle without pain.* It is important to be aware of your own target zone. Stretching at a level below the target zone will not lead to increased flexibility, and stretching above this zone will increase the risk of injury.

5. **Breathing.** Do not hold your breath while stretching. Breathing should be slow, rhythmic, and continuous.

6. **Stretch before and after exercise.** Stretching before vigorous exercise prepares the muscles and joints for activity and reduces the risk of injury. Stretching after vigorous exercise is needed to further stretch the muscles. Both warm-up and cool-down are needed.

INSTRUCTOR DEMONSTRATION

Your course instructor will demonstrate each recommended stretching exercise for volleyball. Observe the demonstration carefully, making note of the performance cues for each exercise.

Shoulder Stretch (triceps)   Elevate one elbow and position your hand straight down your back toward the floor. Reach above your head with your opposite hand and gently apply downward pressure on your elevated elbow.

Photo 1.1
Shoulder stretch

Hold the stretch in the target zone for 15 to 20 seconds and slowly release. Refer to Photo1.1. Repeat this exercise 5 to 8 times with both shoulders.

Lateral Shoulder Stretch Elevate both arms directly overhead and gently stretch toward one side of the body. Bend your hips in the direction of the pull. Knees should be slightly flexed during the exercise. Hold the stretch in the target zone for 15 to 20 seconds and slowly release. Refer to Photo 1.2. Repeat this exercise 5 to 8 times on both sides of the body.

Photo 1.2
Lateral shoulder stretch

Lower Back and Hamstrings Stretch From a standing or sitting position, gently bend forward at the hips and allow the head and arms to hang toward the feet. Have both knees slightly flexed during this exercise. Hold the stretch in the target zone for 15 to 20 seconds and slowly release. Refer to Photo 1.3. Repeat this exercise 5 to 8 times.

Photo 1.3
Lower back and hamstrings stretch

Lower Back and Hip Extensor Stretch From a supine position, elevate one leg toward your chest holding the back of the thigh just under the knee. Apply pressure for the stretch with both arms pulling toward the chest. Hold the stretch in the target zone for 15 to 20 seconds and slowly release. Refer to Photo 1.4. Repeat this exercise 5 to 8 times with each leg.

Photo 1.4
Lower back and hip extensor stretch

Wall Stretch (gastrocnemius) Take a position 2 to 3 feet from a wall or solid structure. Lean forward and support your body weight with your forearms. Flex one leg and position the other leg to the rear with the front foot flat on the floor. Force your hips forward while keeping the back leg straight. Hold the stretch in the target zone for 15 to 20 seconds and slowly release. Refer to Photo 1.5. Repeat this exercise 5 to 8 times with each leg.

Photo 1.5.
Wall stretch

CRITERION TASK 1-1

Performing Stretches: Partner-Checked

Pair up with another person in the class. Perform each stretch while your partner observes for proper technique. Have your partner check and initial below when you have performed each stretch just as your instructor demonstrated. If you have questions or need assistance, use the help signal to alert your instructor.

1. Shoulder stretch
2. Lateral shoulder stretch
3. Lower back and hamstring stretch
4. Lower Back and Hip Extensor Stretch
5. Wall stretch

Partner's initials _____   Date completed _____

MODULE 2

GETTING THE POINT STARTED
UNDERHAND AND OVERHEAD SERVES

INTRODUCTION

Because you can only earn points when your team is serving, it is crucial to learn to serve effectively and consistently. Serves are hit either underhand or overhead. More advanced serves, such as the roundhouse lob serve, topspin serve, and jump serve, are variations of basic underhand and overhead motions. Develop consistency and accuracy before trying to hit powerful serves. Too often beginners attempt to serve the ball powerfully before they master consistency. The result, as you might guess, is simply a missed serve that ends any scoring opportunity.

UNDERHAND SERVE

The basic underhand serve involves the three phases of (1) preparation (preparing to hit the ball), (2) contact (contacting the ball), and (3) follow-through (stroking pattern after contacting the ball).

Note: All instructions are provided for a right-handed player. If you are left-handed, simply exchange the key words "right" and "left."

INSTRUCTOR DEMONSTRATION

Your course instructor will provide you with an explanation and demonstration of the key performance cues for the underhand serve. If you have questions, be sure to ask them before proceeding to the individualized task sequence. Refer to Photos 2.1 through 2.5 as your instructor explains and demonstrates each of the performance cues for the underhand serve.

PERFORMANCE CUES (Preparation Phase)

1. Chest and shoulders face target.
2. Feet apart with left foot slightly forward.
3. Ball held in left hand at waist level.
4. Right hand held open behind ball and facing target.

Photo 2.1
Stance

Photo 2.2
Take back

PERFORMANCE CUES (Contact Phase)

1. Step toward target with left foot.
2. Right hand closes then swings backward and forward into ball with pendulum motion.
3. Left hand releases ball at waist height.
4. Contact ball just below waist level with the heel of your right hand.

Photo 2.3
Contact

PERFORMANCE CUES (Follow-through Phase)

1. Right hand is forcibly raised toward target to impart power to ball.
2. Weight continues to shift forward to left foot.
3. Momentum of step forward and weight shift propels you forward into the court.

Photo 2.4
Postcontact

LEARNING TIPS

1. Start with your body facing the target and your eyes focused on an exact contact spot on the ball.
2. Spread your feet apart, with the left foot slightly forward, so that you can transfer weight toward your target by stepping forward.
3. Hold the ball loosely in your left hand so that you can release, not toss, the ball around waist level.

Photo 2.5
Follow-through

4. Your right hand swings backward and forward into the ball with one continuous movement like the pendulum motion of a clock.
5. Contact the ball with your arm fully extended and the heel of your right
hand striking the bottom of the ball, sending it high across the net.
6. Forcibly strike the ball both upward and outward because a better serve
should land deep in the backcourt of your opponent's court.

   Use the momentum of your weight shift to propel your body forward
into the court to quickly assume a defensive position in the backcourt.

READINESS DRILLS

2-1. *Self-check.* Do all the performance cues discussed in the underhand serve preparation, contact, and follow-through phases.

2-2. *Partner-check.* Take turns demonstrating the proper underhand serving cues as a partner checks for correct form. Repeat this 3 times with each partner providing feedback for correct and incorrect performance cues.

2-3. *Partner serves.* Standing approximately 20 feet from a partner, gently underhand serve the ball 25 times back-and-forth focusing on the correct performance cues. You and your partner should be able to easily catch each serve without moving.

If you experience difficulty with the readiness drills, refer to the **Performance Cues** and review each cue as presented. If you still have difficulty, ask your course instructor to assist you in applying these techniques.

Common Errors and Their Correction

Error	Correction
Ball travels high, but not hard enough to cross net.	Step forward to transfer weight toward target, then contact with heel of hand slightly more in the back, rather than bottom, of the ball.
Ball travels hard, but not high enough to cross net.	Continue to step forward to transfer weight, but then contact with heel of hand slightly more on the bottom, rather than back, of the ball.
Inconsistent trajectory.	Gently release ball from left hand at waist level. DO NOT toss the ball hoping to contact it correctly.

CRITERION TASK 2-1

Underhand Wall Serves for Power: Self-Checked

Take a position approximately 20 feet from the target wall. Place a cone or other marker at that distance. Serve the ball underhand straight toward the wall, aiming to have the ball contact the wall above the target line (approximately net height). Practice this task in blocks of 10 serves. Record the number of successful underhand serves for each block on the **Personal Recording Form.** When three individual block scores reach or exceed 7 out of 10, initial and date in the space provided.

Personal Recording Form									
Block 1	Block 2	Block 3	Block 4	Block 5	Block 6	Block 7	Block 8	Block 9	Block 10
___/10	___/10	___/10	___/10	___/10	___/10	___/10	___/10	___/10	___/10

Your initials _____   Date completed _____

CRITERION TASK 2-2

Underhand Partner Serves for Accuracy: Partner-Checked

Stand with a partner on opposite sides of the net approximately 20 feet from the net. Place a cone or other marker at this distance. (see Illustration 2.1).

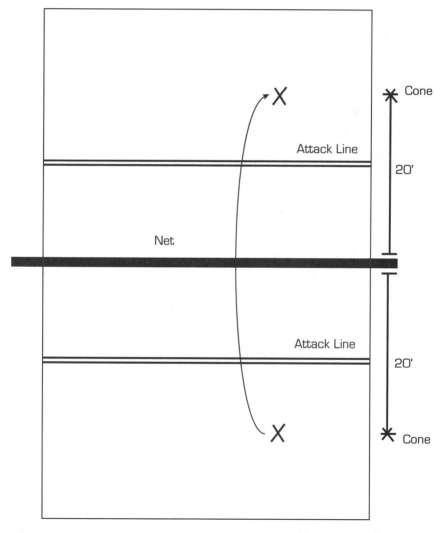

Illustration 2.1
Underhand Partner Serves for Accuracy

Underhand serve the ball straight toward your partner, aiming to have the ball clear the net and land within a couple of feet of your partner. Your partner should be able to catch your serve without moving more than a couple of steps. Practice this task in blocks of 10 serves. Record the number of successful underhand serves caught by your partner without moving more than two steps from his or her starting position for each block on the **Personal Recording Form**. When three individual block scores reach or exceed 7 out of 10, have your partner initial and date in the space provided.

Personal Recording Form									
Block 1	Block 2	Block 3	Block 4	Block 5	Block 6	Block 7	Block 8	Block 9	Block 10
__/10	__/10	__/10	__/10	__/10	__/10	__/10	__/10	__/10	__/10

Your partner's initials _____   Date completed _____

CHALLENGE TASK

Working on consistency, start with a partner, one on each side of the net, near or behind the back boundary. Serve 20 underhand serves across the net and count how many successful serves you complete. A successful serve is one that clears the net and lands in the opposite court. Challenge your partner for the best score.

Your score _____ Percentage _____

Partner score _____ Percentage _____

Note: An accurate and consistent underhand serve is preferred to a powerful, but inaccurate overhead serve. Your instructor may choose to skip the overhead serve at this point so that you may begin practicing the skills needed to rally the ball back and forth across the net.

OVERHEAD SERVE

Although more difficult to perform than the underhand serve, the overhead serve is much more powerful and difficult to return. The basic overhead serve also involves the three phases of (1) preparation, (2) contact, and (3) follow-through. As noted in the introduction, you should develop a consistent and accurate underhand serve before attempting the overhead serve.

INSTRUCTOR DEMONSTRATION

Your course instructor will provide you with an explanation and demonstration of the key performance cues for the overhead serve. If you have questions, be sure to ask them before proceeding to the individualized task sequence. Refer to Photos 2.6 through 2-10 as your instructor explains and demonstrates each performance cue for the overhead serve.

PERFORMANCE CUES (Preparation Phase)

1. Chest and shoulders face target.
2. Feet apart with left foot forward.
3. Ball held in left hand at chest level.
4. Right hand held open.

Photo 2.6
Stance

PERFORMANCE CUES (Contact Phase)

1. Step toward target with left foot.
2. Right hand swings back behind ear with elbow held high.
3. Left hand lifts ball gently high above right shoulder.
4. Contact ball with the heel of your right hand and your arm extended to its highest point.

Photo 2.7
Take back

Photo 2.8
Forward swing

Photo 2.9
Contact

PERFORMANCE CUES (Follow-through Phase)

1. Right hand is forcibly moved toward target with a "punching" motion (very little follow-through) to impart power to ball.
2. Weight continues to shift forward to left foot.
3. Momentum of step forward and weight shift propels you forward into the court.

Photo 2.10
Follow-through

LEARNING TIPS

1. Start with your body facing the target and your eyes focused on an exact contact spot on the ball.
2. Spread your feet apart, with the left foot slightly forward, so that you can transfer weight toward your target by stepping forward.
3. Hold the ball in your left hand with your right hand positioned on top of the ball.
4. Gently lift the ball high enough above your right shoulder so that you can contact the ball with a fully extended arm.
5. Your right hand swings backward toward your ear and then moves forward quickly to impart a "punching" motion to the ball.
6. Contact the ball with your right arm fully extended and the heel of your right hand striking the back of the ball sending it high across the net.
7. Forcibly strike the ball both upward and outward, because a better serve should land deep in the backcourt of your opponent's court.

Use the momentum of your weight shift to propel your body forward into the court to quickly assume a defensive position in the backcourt.

READINESS DRILLS

2-4. *Self-check.* Do all the performance cues discussed in the overhead serve preparation, contact, and follow-through phases.

2-5. *Partner-check.* Take turns demonstrating the proper overhead serving cues as a partner checks for correct form. Repeat this 3 times with each partner.

2-6. *Partner Serves.* Standing approximately 20 feet from a partner, gently overhead serve the ball 25 times back and forth, focusing on the correct performance cues. You and your partner should be able to easily catch each serve without moving.

If you experience difficulty with the readiness drills, refer to the **Performance Cues** and review each cue as presented. If you still have difficulty, ask your course instructor to assist you in applying these techniques.

Common Errors and Their Correction

Error	Correction
Ball travels high, but not hard enough to cross net.	Lift ball slightly more toward the net, step forward to transfer weight toward target, then contact with heel of hand slightly more in the back, rather than bottom, of the ball.
Ball travels hard, but not high enough to cross net.	Lift ball slightly closer to your body, continue to step forward to transfer weight, but then contact with heel of hand slightly more on the bottom, rather than back, of ball.
Inconsistent trajectory.	Gently lift the ball from left hand at chest level; DO NOT toss the ball wildly hoping to contact it correctly.

CRITERION TASK 2-3 (Optional)

Overhead Wall Serves for Power: Self-Checked

Take a position approximately 20 feet from the target wall. Place a cone or other marker at that distance. Serve the ball overhead straight toward the wall, aiming to have the ball contact the wall above the target line (approximately net height). Practice this task in blocks of 10 serves. Record the number of successful overhead serves for each block on the **Personal Recording Form**. When three individual block scores reach or exceed 7 out of 10, initial and date in the space provided.

Personal Recording Form									
Block 1	Block 2	Block 3	Block 4	Block 5	Block 6	Block 7	Block 8	Block 9	Block 10
___/10	___/10	___/10	___/10	___/10	___/10	___/10	___/10	___/10	___/10

Your initials _____ Date completed _____

CRITERION TASK 2-4 (Optional)

Overhead Partner Serves for Accuracy: Partner-Checked

Stand with a partner on opposite sides of the net approximately 20 feet from the net. Place a cone or other marker at that distance (see Illustration 2.2).

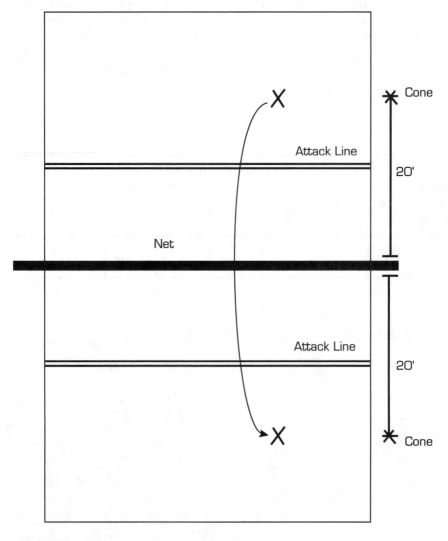

Illustration 2.2
Overhead Partner Serves for Accuracy

Overhead serve the ball straight toward your partner, aiming to have the ball clear the net and land within a couple of feet of your partner. Practice this task in blocks of 10 serves. Record the number of successful overhead serves caught by your partner without moving more than two steps from his or her starting position for each block on the Personal Recording Form. When three individual block scores reach or exceed 6 out of 10, have your partner initial and date in the space provided.

Personal Recording Form									
Block 1	Block 2	Block 3	Block 4	Block 5	Block 6	Block 7	Block 8	Block 9	Block 10
___/10	___/10	___/10	___/10	___/10	___/10	___/10	___/10	___/10	___/10

Your partner's initials _____   Date completed _____

CHALLENGE TASK

Working on consistency, start with a partner, one on each side of the net near or behind the back boundary. Serve 20 overhead serves across the net and count how many successful serves you complete. A successful serve is one that clears the net and lands in the opposite court. Challenge your partner for the best score.

Your score _____ Percentage _____.

Partner's score _____ Percentage _____.

INSTRUCTOR CHECK

Upon completion of this module, contact your instructor to evaluate your underhand and/or overhead serve. Have your course instructor place her or

his initials here _____ when you have successfully completed this evaluation.

This module was completed on _____ (date).

MODULE **3**

SETTING-UP THE POINT
UNDERHAND AND OVERHEAD PASSING

INTRODUCTION

Passing in volleyball refers to the way in which a team moves the ball into position to make an offensive shot to the opponents' side of the court, preferably with a spike. Two types of passes are used to get the ball into position, the underhand pass and the overhead pass. Typically, the underhand pass is used to receive the ball on your side of the net and move it to a designated *setter*, who uses the overhead pass to set the ball to the spiker at the net. This bump–set–spike sequence is the foundation of offensive strategy in volleyball.

UNDERHAND PASS

The **underhand pass**, more commonly called the **bump**, is the most basic skill needed to pass the ball to a teammate, usually the setter. Effectively passing the ball, especially when returning a serve, is critical for beginning your offensive attack. The underhand pass involves the three phases of (1) preparation, (2) contact, and (3) follow-through.

*Note: Several tasks in this module can be completed by yourself or with a partner. Later you will need to work in small groups.

INSTRUCTOR DEMONSTRATION

Your course instructor will provide you with an explanation and demonstration of the key performance cues for the underhand pass. If you have questions, be sure to ask them before proceeding to the individualized task sequence. Refer to Photos 3.1 through 3.5 as your instructor explains and demonstrates each of the performance cues for the underhand pass.

PERFORMANCE CUES (Preparation Phase)

1. Move quickly to receiving position (knees bent, feet shoulder width apart, or one foot slightly forward, facing target).
2. Hands joined with elbows rotated inward (forming a *platform* with forearms to contact ball).
3. Keep knees bent to absorb force of ball.

Photo 3.1
Receiving position

Photo 3.2
Moving to the ball

PERFORMANCE CUES (Contact Phase)

1. Eyes follow ball to platform.
2. Contact ball with platform slanted toward target.
3. *Do not swing arms toward target;* rather lift the platform with extension of legs at contact.
4. Try to keep your platform as level (parallel to thighs) as possible.
5. Contact ball just below, or at, waist level.

Photo 3.3
Contact, side view

Photo 3.4
Contact, front view

PERFORMANCE CUES (Follow-through Phase)

1. Platform gently moves toward target.
2. Keep hands joined throughout follow-through.
3. Eyes follow ball to target.

Photo 3.5
Follow-through

LEARNING TIPS

1. Start with your body facing the server in a proper receiving position (knees bent, feet shoulder width apart or one foot slightly forward).
2. Keep hands joined with elbows rotated inward (forming a *platform* with forearms to contact ball) throughout pass.
3. Eyes follow ball to platform; then eyes follow ball toward target.
4. Platform is slanted toward target, rather than swinging arms toward target.
5. Absorb force and guide ball toward target with a slight extension of legs at contact.
6. Contact ball just below, or at, waist level.
7. Keep hands joined throughout follow-through.

READINESS DRILLS

3-1. *Self-check.* Do all the performance cues discussed in the underhand pass preparation, contact, and follow-through phases.

3-2. *Partner-check.* Take turns demonstrating the proper underhand pass cues as a partner checks for correct form. Repeat this 3 times with each partner.

3-3. *Partner Bumps.* Standing approximately 10 feet apart, have your partner gently toss the ball to you; then gently bump the ball back to your partner's hands, focusing on the correct performance cues. You and your partner should be able to catch each bump without moving.

If you experience difficulty with the readiness drills, refer to the **Performance Cues** and review each cue as presented. If you still have difficulty, ask your course instructor to assist you in applying these techniques.

Common Errors and Their Correction

Error	Correction
Ball travels wildly with arms separating.	Keep hands connected throughout contact and follow-through.
Arms follow through above shoulders.	Extension of legs, not swinging of arms, provides power. Keep arms below shoulders on follow through.
Inconsistent trajectory off platform.	Platform needs to be flat (arms not separated) at contact. Contact ball equally with both forearms.

CRITERION TASK 3-1

Underhand Pass Air Dribbling: Self-Checked

Find an open space in the practice area. With a ball of your own, toss the ball upward and gently bump it continuously to yourself. Try to bump the ball to approximately net height each time. Practice this task in blocks of 10 passes. Record the number of successful passes for each block on the **Personal Recording Form**. When three individual block scores reach or exceed 6 out of 10, initial and date in the space provided.

Personal Recording Form									
Block 1	Block 2	Block 3	Block 4	Block 5	Block 6	Block 7	Block 8	Block 9	Block 10
___/10	___/10	___/10	___/10	___/10	___/10	___/10	___/10	___/10	___/10

Your initials _____   Date completed _____

CRITERION TASK 3-2 (Optional)

Underhand Pass Air/Court Dribble: Self-Checked

Find an open space in the practice area. With a ball of your own, toss the ball upward and gently bump it skyward; let it bounce off the floor and then bump it upward again. Try to bump the ball just above the top of the net each time. Practice this task in blocks of 10 passes. Record the number of successful passes for each block on the **Personal Recording Form**. When three individual block scores reach or exceed 6 out of 10, initial and date in the space provided.

Personal Recording Form									
Block 1	Block 2	Block 3	Block 4	Block 5	Block 6	Block 7	Block 8	Block 9	Block 10
___/10	___/10	___/10	___/10	___/10	___/10	___/10	___/10	___/10	___/10

Your initials _____   Date completed _____

CRITERION TASK 3-3

Underhand Pass from Toss: Partner-Checked

In a group of three, have one partner stand on the opposite side of the net and the other in the middle frontcourt (next to the net) on your side (see Illustration 3.1).

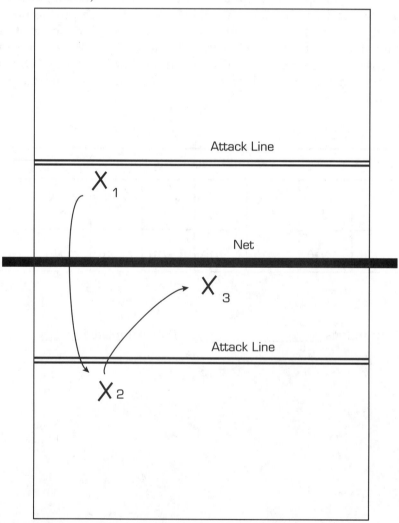

Illustration 3.1
Underhand Pass (Bump) from Toss

Your first partner (1) will *toss* the ball over the net straight toward you (2). Gently bump the ball to your second partner (3), aiming to have the ball land within two steps of his or her position. Practice this task in blocks of 10 passes. Record the number of successful passes caught by your partner without moving more that two steps from his/her starting position for each block on the **Personal Recording Form**. When three individual block scores reach or exceed 7 out of 10, have your partner initial and date in the space provided.

Personal Recording Form									
Block 1	Block 2	Block 3	Block 4	Block 5	Block 6	Block 7	Block 8	Block 9	Block 10
___/10	___/10	___/10	___/10	___/10	___/10	___/10	___/10	___/10	___/10

Your partner's initials _____ Date completed _____

CRITERION TASK 3-4

Underhand Pass from Serve: Partner-Checked

In a group of three, have one partner stand at the opposite boundary and the other in the middle frontcourt (next to the net) on your side (see Illustration 3.2).

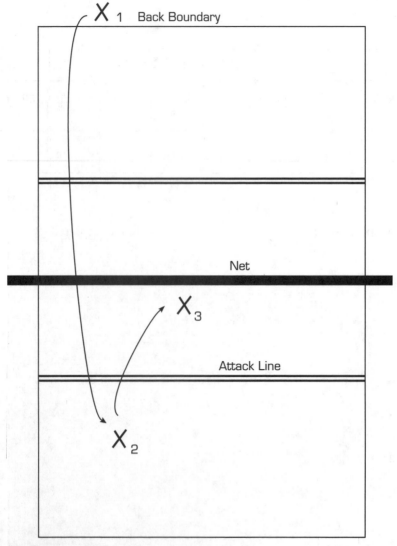

Illustration 3.2
Underhand Pass (Bump) from Serve

Your first partner (1) will *underhand serve* the ball over the net straight toward you (2). Gently bump the ball to your second partner, (3) aiming to have the ball land within two steps of his or her position. Practice this task in blocks of 10 passes. Record the number of successful passes caught by your partner without moving more that two steps from his or her starting position for each block on the **Personal Recording Form**. When three individual block scores reach or exceed 6 out of 10, have your partner initial and date in the space provided.

Personal Recording Form									
Block 1	Block 2	Block 3	Block 4	Block 5	Block 6	Block 7	Block 8	Block 9	Block 10
___/10	___/10	___/10	___/10	___/10	___/10	___/10	___/10	___/10	___/10

Your partner's initials _____ Date completed _____

OVERHEAD PASS

The **overhead pass**, more commonly called the **set**, is a more advanced skill used to pass the ball to a teammate, most often one who is getting ready for a spike. Effectively passing the ball with the overhead pass, especially after a bump, is critical for finishing your offensive attack. The overhead pass involves the three phases of (1) preparation, (2) contact, and (3) follow-through.

INSTRUCTOR DEMONSTRATION

Your course instructor will provide you with an explanation and demonstration of the key performance cues for the overhead pass. If you have questions, be sure to ask them before proceeding to the individualized task sequence. Refer to Photos 3.6 through 3.10 as your instructor explains and demonstrates each performance cue for the overhead pass.

PERFORMANCE CUES (Preparation Phase)

1. Move quickly to the receiving position (knees bent, feet shoulder width apart, or one foot slightly forward, facing target).
2. Hands placed in front of forehead (forming a *window* with thumbs and index fingers).
3. Eyes watch for ball by looking through window.

Photo 3.6
Receiving position

PERFORMANCE CUES (Contact Phase)

1. Eyes follow ball to window.
2. Contact ball with window pointing toward target.
3. *Do not punch hands toward ball*; rather, gently push the ball with fingertips.

Photo 3.7
Contact, front view

Photo 3.8
Contact, back view

Photo 3.9
Post-contact

PERFORMANCE CUES (Follow-through Phase)

1. Window moves toward target by extending fingers.
2. Eyes follow ball to target.

Photo 3.10
Follow-through

LEARNING TIPS

1. Start with your body facing the passer in a proper receiving position (knees bent, feet shoulder width apart or one foot slightly forward).
2. Keep hands in front of forehead, forming a *window* with thumbs and index fingers.
3. Eyes look for ball through window.
4. Window is pointed toward target, with extension of fingertips providing force needed to guide ball to the target.
5. Absorb force and push ball without "slapping" ball with palms of hands.

READINESS DRILLS

3-4. *Self-check.* Do all the performance cues discussed in the overhead pass preparation, contact, and follow-through phases.

3-5. *Partner-check.* Take turns demonstrating the proper overhead pass cues as a partner checks for correct form. Repeat this demonstration or drill 3 times with each partner.

3-6. *Partner Sets.* Standing approximately 10 feet apart, have your partner gently toss the ball to you; return the ball with an overhead pass to your partner's hands, focusing on the correct performance cues. You and your partner should be able to catch each pass without moving more than two steps from your original spot.

If you experience difficulty with the readiness drills, refer to the **Performance Cues** and review each cue as presented. If you still have difficulty, ask your course instructor to assist you in applying these techniques.

Common Errors and Their Correction

Error	Correction
Ball is "slapped" with palms of hands.	Spread fingers to cushion ball and extend fingers quickly to target for power.
Ball is "held" or "carried."	Spread fingers and cushion ball with fingers only (not palms).
Inconsistent trajectory and excess spin.	Point chest and shoulders to target. Impart force to ball equally between hands.

CRITERION TASK 3-5

Overhead Pass Air Dribbling: Self-Checked

Find an open space in the practice area. With a ball of your own, toss the ball upward and gently set it continuously to yourself. Try to set the ball to approximately net height each time. Practice this task in blocks of 10 passes. Record the number of successful passes for each block on the **Personal Recording Form**. When three individual block scores reach or exceed 6 out of 10, initial and date in the space provided.

Personal Recording Form									
Block 1	Block 2	Block 3	Block 4	Block 5	Block 6	Block 7	Block 8	Block 9	Block 10
___/10	___/10	___/10	___/10	___/10	___/10	___/10	___/10	___/10	___/10

Your initials _____   Date completed _____

CRITERION TASK 3-6 (Optional)

Overhead Pass Air/Court Dribble: Self-Checked

Find an open space in the practice area. With a ball of your own, toss the ball upward and gently set it skyward; let it bounce off the floor and then set it upward again. Try to set the ball just above the top of the net each time. Practice this task in blocks of 10 passes. Record the number of successful passes for each block on the **Personal Recording Form**. When three individual block scores reach or exceed 6 out of 10, initial and date in the space provided.

Personal Recording Form									
Block 1	Block 2	Block 3	Block 4	Block 5	Block 6	Block 7	Block 8	Block 9	Block 10
___/10	___/10	___/10	___/10	___/10	___/10	___/10	___/10	___/10	___/10

Your initials _____   Date completed _____

CRITERION TASK 3-7

Overhead Pass from Toss: Partner-Checked

In a group of three on the same side of the net, have one partner stand in the backcourt and the other in the frontcourt toward the sideline (see Illustration 3.3).

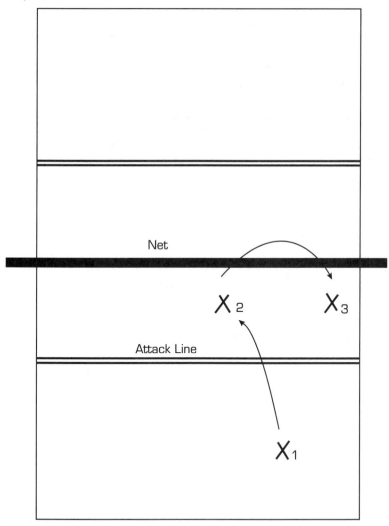

Illustration 3.3
Overhead Pass (Set) from Toss

    Your backcourt partner (1) will toss the ball upward straight toward you (2). Set the ball to your frontcourt partner (3), aiming to have the ball travel 2 to 3 feet higher than the top of the net and land within two steps of his or her position. Record the number of successful passes caught by your partner without moving more that two steps from his or her starting position for each block on the **Personal Recording Form**. When three individual block scores reach or exceed 7 out of 10, have your partner initial and date in the space provided.

Personal Recording Form									
Block 1	Block 2	Block 3	Block 4	Block 5	Block 6	Block 7	Block 8	Block 9	Block 10
___/10	___/10	___/10	___/10	___/10	___/10	___/10	___/10	___/10	___/10

Your partner's initials _____   Date completed _____

CRITERION TASK 3-8

Overhead Pass from Underhand Pass: Instructor-Checked

In a group of three on the same side of the net, have one partner stand in the backcourt and the other in the frontcourt toward the sideline (see Illustration 3.4).

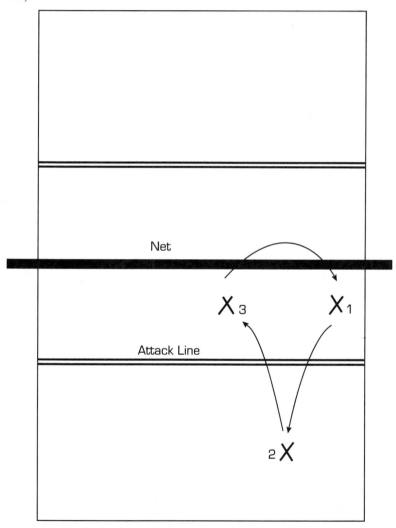

Illustration 3.4
Overhead Pass (Set) from Underhand Pass

Your frontcourt partner (1) will toss the ball upward toward your backcourt partner (2), who will underhand pass the ball to you (3). Set the ball over to your frontcourt partner, aiming to have the ball travel 2 to 3 feet higher than the top of the net and land within one step of his or her position. Practice this task in blocks of 10 passes. Record the number of successful passes caught by your partner without moving more than one step from his or her starting position for each block on the **Personal Recording Form**. When three individual block scores reach or exceed 6 out of 10, have your instructor initial and date in the space provided.

Personal Recording Form									
Block 1	Block 2	Block 3	Block 4	Block 5	Block 6	Block 7	Block 8	Block 9	Block 10
__/10	__/10	__/10	__/10	__/10	__/10	__/10	__/10	__/10	__/10

Your instructor's initials _____   Date completed _____

CHALLENGE TASK

In a group of four, with one partner on the other side of the set in a serving position and three partners on the same side of the net; serve (1), bump (2), then set (3) the ball to the frontcourt player (4), who hits the ball over the net with either a bump or set back toward the server (see Illustration 3.5).

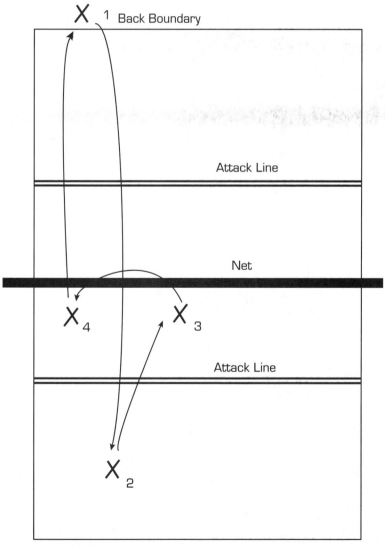

Illustration 3.5
Combination of Serve, Bump, and Set

This small-group activity requires teamwork. Do this task for 15 minutes. Count how many successful three-hit combinations (serve, bump, set) your team can complete.

Team score _____

INSTRUCTOR CHECK

Upon completion of this module, contact your instructor to evaluate your underhand and overhead passing. Have your course instructor place her or

his initials here _____ when you have successfully completed this evaluation.

This module was completed on _____ (date).

MODULE 4

PLAYING OFFENSE
DINKING AND SPIKING

INTRODUCTION

To win points in volleyball, your offensive skills need persistent practice and teamwork. The two basic offensive shots are the **dink** and the **spike**. Both are variations of the same basic overhead motion. Because of the difficulty associated with the spike (that is, jumping as high as possible and hitting a moving object over a net), the dink should be mastered with consistency and accuracy before trying the spike.

DINK

The **dink** can be used by players who cannot jump high enough to spike the ball. The purpose of this shot is to draw your opponents into the air at the net and then softly lift the ball over their outstretched arms or to a vacant spot on the court. It is most effective when you have hit several spikes in a row and the defense is anticipating that you will spike it again, opening up spaces in the defense. The dink involves the three phases of (1) preparation, (2) contact, and (3) follow-through.

INSTRUCTOR DEMONSTRATION

Your course instructor will provide you with an explanation and demonstration of the key performance cues for the dink. If you have questions, be sure to ask them before proceeding to the individualized task sequence. Refer to Photos 4.1 through 4.5 as your instructor explains and demonstrates each performance cue for the overhead dink.

PERFORMANCE CUES (Preparation Phase)

1. Wait for set by standing on the attack line (the line 9 feet 10 inches from net)
2. Begin approach to net when set is hit in your direction.
3. Using several small steps to position yourself, jump off both feet toward ball.

Photo 4.1
Approach

Photo 4.2
Setup for jump

PERFORMANCE CUES (Contact Phase)

1. Use both arms to extend your body toward the ball.
2. Contact ball with your right arm extended to its highest point using the fingertips of your right hand.

Photo 4.3
Jump

Photo 4.4
Contact

PERFORMANCE CUES (Follow-through Phase)

1. Right hand follows ball to target.
2. Land on both feet with bent knees to cushion landing.
3. Immediately assume a defensive position at the net in preparation of your opponent's counterattack.

Photo 4.5
Follow-through

LEARNING TIPS

1. Stand on the attack line waiting for the set.
2. Approach the net as the set is hit in your direction.
3. Use small steps to position yourself; then jump off both feet toward ball.
4. Use both arms to extend your body toward the ball.
5. Use your fingertips to contact the ball, with your right arm extended.
6. Your right hand follows ball toward target.
7. Land on both feet with bent knees to cushion landing.
8. Immediately assume a defensive position.

READINESS DRILLS

4-1. *Self-check.* Do all the performance cues discussed in the overhead dink preparation, contact, and follow-through phases.

4-2. *Partner-check.* Take turns demonstrating the proper overhead dink cues as a partner checks for correct form. Repeat this three times with each partner.

If you experience difficulty with the readiness drills refer to the **Performance Cues** and review each cue as presented. If you still have difficulty, ask your course instructor to assist you in applying these techniques.

Common Errors and Their Correction

Error	Correction
Ball travels high over blocker, but gives opponents too much time to react.	Gently tap the ball just high enough to clear the blocker by contacting the ball more on the back, rather than the bottom.
Ball travels too low, hitting net, or is blocked back into own court.	Gently tap the ball high enough to clear the blocker by contacting the ball more on the bottom, rather than back.
Ball travels over blocker and quickly falls to court, but offensive player runs into the net.	Set must be away (1 to 3 feet) from the net, and offensive player must jump off both feet, reaching toward ceiling, rather than jumping forward toward net

CRITERION TASK 4-1

Overhead Dink from Toss: Partner-Checked

In a group of three, take a position next to the net with one partner in a blocking position on the opposite side of the net and your other partner in the frontcourt setting position (see Illustration 4.1).

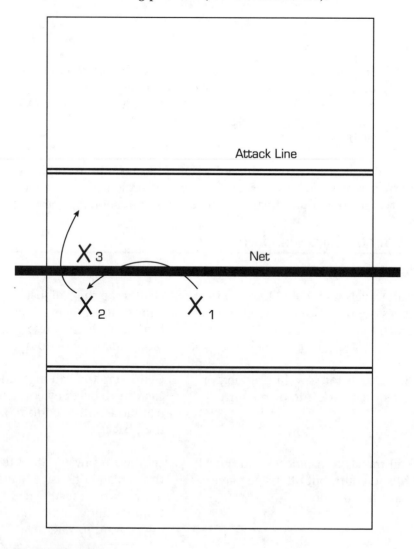

Illustration 4.1
Dink from Toss

Your partner (1) tosses the ball underhand, mimicking an overhead set to you (2). Jump upward to the ball and attempt to dink the ball over the outstretched hands of the blocker (3). Practice the dink in blocks of 10. Record the number of successful dinks for each block on the **Personal Recording Form**. When three individual block scores reach or exceed 7 out of 10, initial and date in the space provided.

Personal Recording Form									
Block 1	Block 2	Block 3	Block 4	Block 5	Block 6	Block 7	Block 8	Block 9	Block 10
__/10	__/10	__/10	__/10	__/10	__/10	__/10	__/10	__/10	__/10

Your partner's initials _____ Date completed _____

CRITERION TASK 4-2

Overhead Dink from Set: Partner-Checked

In a group of three, take a position at the attack line with one partner in a blocking position on the opposite side of the net and your other partner in the frontcourt setting position (see Illustration 4.2).

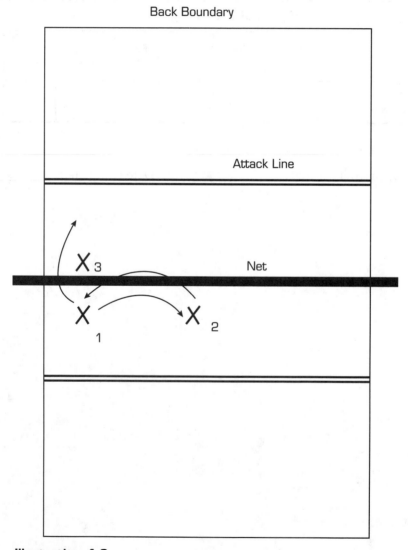

Illustration 4.2
Dink from Overhead Set

Begin with a ball in your hands (1). Toss the ball underhand toward your frontcourt partner (2), who then sets the ball 2 to 3 feet above the net and 1 to 3 feet from the net. After tossing the ball, get ready to approach the net to dink the ball over the outstretched hands of the blocker (3). Practice the dink in blocks of 10. Record the number of successful dinks for each block on the **Personal Recording Form**. When three individual block scores reach or exceed 6 out of 10, have your partner initial and date in the space provided.

Personal Recording Form									
Block 1	Block 2	Block 3	Block 4	Block 5	Block 6	Block 7	Block 8	Block 9	Block 10
__/10	__/10	__/10	__/10	__/10	__/10	__/10	__/10	__/10	__/10

Your partner's initials _____   Date completed _____

SPIKE

The **spike** is the most effective offensive shot in volleyball. It requires a combination of jumping ability, timing, and power. Its purpose is to hit the ball down into the court or at a defensive player who cannot handle it, resulting in a side-out or a point. Many beginning players may not be able to spike because they cannot jump high enough to clear the net and hit down on the ball. The spike also involves the three phases of (1) preparation, (2) contact, and (3) follow-through. The major difference between the dink and the spike is the force imparted to the ball and the contact point on the ball. While the dink is hit gently by striking the bottom part of the ball, the spike is hit very hard by striking the back of the ball and driving it downward into the court.

Note: *Similar to the overhead serve, your instructor may choose to skip the spike at this time so that you may begin practicing the other skills needed to rally back and forth across the net.*

INSTRUCTOR DEMONSTRATION

Your course instructor will provide you with an explanation and demonstration of the key performance cues for the spike. If you have questions, be sure to ask them before proceeding to the individualized task sequence. Refer to Photos 4.6 through 4.10 as your instructor explains and demonstrates each of the performance cues for the overhead spike.

PERFORMANCE CUES (Preparation Phase)

1. Wait for the set by standing on the attack line.
2. Begin your approach to the net when the set is hit in your direction.
3. Using several small steps to position yourself, jump off both feet toward ball.

Photo 4.6
Approach for spike

Photo 4.7
Setup for jump

PERFORMANCE CUES (Contact Phase)

1. Use both arms to extend your body toward the ball.
2. Swing arm forward like an overhead serve.
3. Contact ball in front of your right shoulder with arm extended and ball contacted with the heel of your hand.

Photo 4.8
Jump

Photo 4.9
Contact

PERFORMANCE CUES (Follow-through Phase)

1. Right hand forcibly follows ball to target.
2. Land on both feet with bent knees to cushion landing.
3. Immediately assume a defensive position at the net in preparation of your opponent's counterattack.

Photo 4.10
Follow-through

LEARNING TIPS

1. Stand on the attack line waiting for the set.
2. Approach net as set is hit in your direction.
3. Use small steps to position yourself; then jump off both feet toward ball.
4. Use both arms to extend your body toward the ball.
5. Use the heel of your hand to contact the ball, with your right arm extended in an overhead serving motion. Your right hand forcibly follows ball toward target.
6. Land on both feet with bent knees to cushion landing.
7. Immediately assume a defensive position.

READINESS DRILLS

4-3. *Self-check.* Do all the performance cues discussed in the overhead spike preparation, contact, and follow-through phases.
4-4. *Partner-check.* Take turns demonstrating the proper overhead spike cues as a partner checks for correct form. Repeat this 3 times with each partner.

  If you experience difficulty with the readiness drills, refer to the **Performance Cues** and review each cue as presented. If you still have difficulty, ask your course instructor to assist you in applying these techniques.

Common Errors and Their Correction

Error	**Correction**
Ball travels high over blocker, but lands beyond the court boundary.	Forcibly strike the back of the ball, driving it downward.
Ball travels too, low hitting net or is blocked back into own court.	Continue to forcibly strike the back of the ball, but do not let the ball drop too far downward from the set. Also, aim the spike away from an aggressive blocker by aiming crosscourt or down-the-line.
Ball travels over blocker and quickly falls to court, but offensive player runs into the net.	Set must be away (1 to 3 feet) from the net, and offensive player must jump off both feet, reaching toward ceiling, rather than jumping forward toward net.

CRITERION TASK 4-3

Overhead Spike into Wall: Self-Checked

Stand approximately 10 feet from the wall with one ball. Mark this distance with a cone or other marker (see Illustration 4.3).

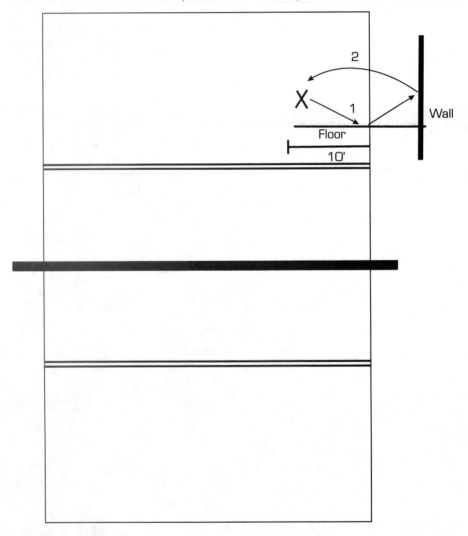

Illustration 4.3
Spike into Wall

Toss the ball upward, mimicking an overhead set, and forcibly spike the ball into the floor, rebounding off the wall back to you. Continue by respiking the ball repeatedly. Practice the spike in blocks of 10. Record the number of successful spikes for each block on the **Personal Recording Form**. When three individual block scores reach or exceed 6 out of 10, initial and date in the space provided.

Personal Recording Form									
Block 1	Block 2	Block 3	Block 4	Block 5	Block 6	Block 7	Block 8	Block 9	Block 10
___/10	___/10	___/10	___/10	___/10	___/10	___/10	___/10	___/10	___/10

Your initials _____   Date completed _____

CRITERION TASK 4-4 (Optional)

Overhead Spike from Set: Partner-Checked

In a group of three, take a position at the attack line, with one partner in a blocking position on the opposite side of the net and your other partner in the frontcourt setting position (see Illustration 4.4).

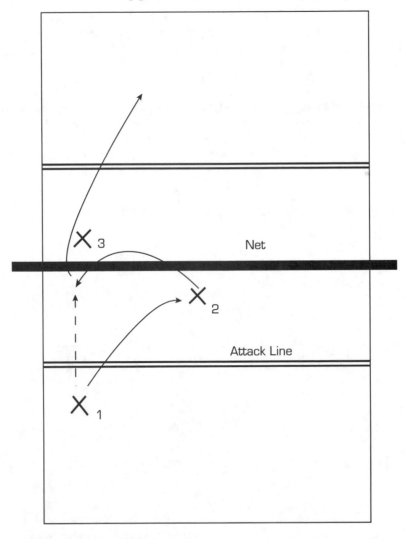

Illustration 4.4
Spike from Overhead Set

Begin with the ball in your hands (1). Toss the ball underhand to your frontcourt partner (2), who then sets the ball 2 to 3 feet above the net and 1 to 3 feet from the net. After tossing the ball, get ready to approach the ball to spike it over or around the outstretched hands of the blocker (3). Practice the spike in blocks of 10. Record the number of successful spikes for each block on the **Personal Recording Form**. When three individual block scores reach or exceed 6 out of 10, have your partner initial and date in the space provided.

Personal Recording Form									
Block 1	Block 2	Block 3	Block 4	Block 5	Block 6	Block 7	Block 8	Block 9	Block 10
___/10	___/10	___/10	___/10	___/10	___/10	___/10	___/10	___/10	___/10

Your partner's initials _____   Date completed _____

CHALLENGE TASK

In a group of four, with one partner on the other side of the set in a serving position and three partners on the same side of the net, serve (1), bump (2), then set (3) the ball to the frontcourt player (4), who hits the ball over the net with either a dink or spike toward the server (see Illustration 4.5).

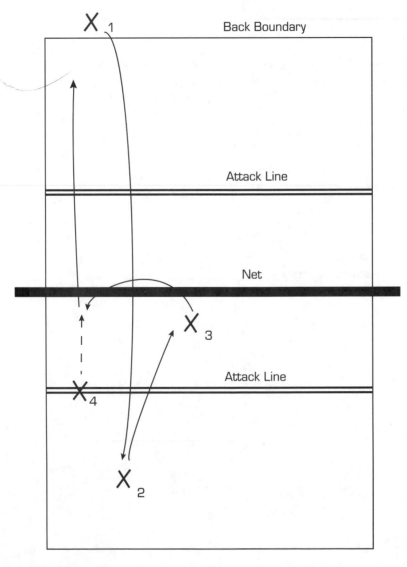

Illustration 4.5
Combination of Serve, Bump, Set, and Dink/Spike

This small-group activity requires teamwork. Do this task for 15 minutes. Count the highest number of successful four-hit combinations (serve, bump, set, dink/spike) that your team can complete.

Team score ————————————

INSTRUCTOR CHECK

Upon completion of this module, contact your instructor to evaluate your dink and spike. Have your course instructor place her or his initials here _____ when you have successfully completed this evaluation.

This module was completed on _____ (date).

MODULE 5

PLAYING DEFENSE
BLOCKING AND DIGGING

INTRODUCTION

Volleyball play will have very quick transitions from offense to defense in most points. As one team has the ball on their side of the net, the defensive team must anticipate and move into the best position to return the spike, dink, or free ball that will come to them from the other team. The two basic defensive shots are the **block** and the **dig**. The block is the first line of defense as one or more players attempt to deflect the opponent's dink or spike back into their court. When the block is not successful, the defensive team must use the dig to receive the ball in its court, beginning their own offensive sequence.

*Note: Because of the jumping skill needed to successfully block, your instructor may choose to skip the block at this time so that you may begin practicing the dig in order to hasten your ability to rally back and forth across the net.

BLOCK

The **block** can be made by one or more players, all using the same technique to form a "wall" that the spike must penetrate or be hit around. The first purpose of the block is actually an offensive one; the most effective block will deflect the spike back into the opponents' court in a way that is not playable. The second purpose of the block is to force the spiking opponent into "going around" it and hitting a shot directly to a ready defender. The spike involves the three phases of (1) preparation, (2) contact, and (3) follow-through.

INSTRUCTOR DEMONSTRATION

Your course instructor will provide you with an explanation and demonstration of the key performance cues for the block. If you have questions, be sure to ask them before proceeding to the individualized task sequence. Refer to Photos 5.1 through 5.3 as your instructor explains and demonstrates each performance cue for the block.

PERFORMANCE CUES (Preparation Phase)

1. Wait at net watching opposing setter.
2. Keep hands at shoulder level.
3. After you see the set in the opposite court, immediately identify and focus on the opposing hitter.

Photo 5.1
Setup

PERFORMANCE CUES (Contact Phase)

1. Position yourself in front on the hitter.
2. Jump immediately after the hitter jumps.
3. Reach hands above the top of the net to deflect ball. DO NOT TOUCH THE NET.

Photo 5.2
Contact, front view

Photo 5.3
Contact, back view

PERFORMANCE CUES (Follow-through Phase)

1. Move your hands and arms over the net to deflect the ball downward into the opponents' court.
2. Land on both feet with bent knees to cushion landing.
3. Immediately turn away from net in preparation for your team's offensive attack.

LEARNING TIPS

1. Wait at net, watching opposing setter to determine direction of attack.
2. Keep hands at shoulder level in case you need to jump and block quickly.
3. After you see the set in the opposite court, immediately identify and focus on the opposing hitter.
4. Slide in the direction of the hitter to position yourself in front on the hitter's dominant attacking shoulder.
5. Time your jump so that you jump immediately *after* the hitter jumps.
6. Reach hands as high as possible above the top of the net to deflect ball downward back into your opponent's court.
7. Land on both feet with bent knees to cushion landing.
8. If the ball deflects off your hands into your team's court, immediately turn away from net in preparation for your team's offensive attack.

READINESS DRILLS

5-1. *Self-check.* Do all the performance cues discussed in the block preparation, contact, and follow-through phases.
5-2. *Partner-check.* Take turns demonstrating the proper block cues as a partner checks for correct form. Repeat this 3 times with each partner.

If you experience difficulty with the readiness drills, refer to the **Performance Cues** and review each cue as presented. If you still have difficulty, ask your course instructor to assist you in applying these techniques.

Common Errors and Their Correction

Error	Correction
Ball travels over your block.	Jump as high as possible, but also jump *after* your opposing hitter does. If you jump at the same time, you will be descending as the ball travels over your outstretched hands.
Ball travels off your block out of bounds or hits you in the head.	Jump as high as possible, but also *immediately after* your opposing hitter does. If you jump too late, you will be ascending as the ball is traveling downward. The result is often a deflected ball traveling out of bounds or hitting you in the head.
You block the ball successfully, but run into the net.	Jump straight upward, reaching your hands as high as possible. You must jump off both feet. reaching toward ceiling, rather than jumping forward toward net.

CRITERION TASK 5-1

Blocks of Toss: Partner-Checked

In a group of three, take a position next to the net, with two partners in hitting and setting positions on the opposite side of the net. Your partners will simulate a set and hit by tossing the ball overhand into your court. Jump upward and attempt to block the ball into the tosser's court. Practice this task in blocks of 10. Record the number of successful blocks on the **Personal Recording Form**. When three individual scores reach or exceed 7 out of 10, have your partner initial and date in the space provided.

Personal Recording Form									
Block 1	Block 2	Block 3	Block 4	Block 5	Block 6	Block 7	Block 8	Block 9	Block 10
___/10	___/10	___/10	___/10	___/10	___/10	___/10	___/10	___/10	___/10

Your partner's initials _____   Date completed _____

CRITERION TASK 5-2

Blocks of Overhead Dink/Spike: Partner Checked

In a group of three, take a position next to the net with two partners in hitting and setting positions on the opposite side of the net (see Illustration 5.1).

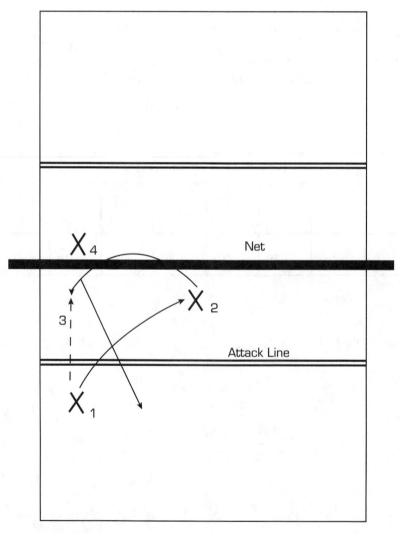

Illustration 5.1
Block of Overhead Dink/Spike

Your partners will complete a set (1, 2, 3) and spike/dink into your court. You (4) jump upward and attempt to block the ball into the hitter's court. Practice this task in blocks of 10. Record the number of successful blocks on the **Personal Recording Form**. When three individual scores reach or exceed 5 out of 10, have your partner initial and date in the space provided

Personal Recording Form									
Block 1	Block 2	Block 3	Block 4	Block 5	Block 6	Block 7	Block 8	Block 9	Block 10
___/10	___/10	___/10	___/10	___/10	___/10	___/10	___/10	___/10	___/10

Your partner's initials _____ Date completed _____

DIG

The **dig** is used to return a spike that does not hit the block. The spiked ball will be coming very hard, so the dig is a difficult skill to master. The purpose of the dig is to handle the spiked ball in a way that allows the receiving team to control it and begin its own offensive sequence. The dig involves the three phases of (1) preparation, (2) contact, and (3) follow-through. The major difference between the dig and the block is the court position and contact point. Whereas the block is hit with arms outstretched close to the net, the dig is played underhand (very similar to a bump) from the backcourt or just behind the blockers.

INSTRUCTOR DEMONSTRATION

Your course instructor will provide you with an explanation and demonstration of the key performance cues for the dig. If you have questions, be sure to ask them before proceeding to the individualized task sequence. Refer to Photos 5.4 through 5.6 as your instructor explains and demonstrates each performance cue for the dig.

PERFORMANCE CUES (Preparation Phase)

1. Move quickly to the receiving position (knees bent, feet shoulder width apart, or one foot slightly forward, facing target).
2. Hands joined with elbows rotated inward (forming a *platform* with forearms to contact ball).
3. Keep knees bent to absorb force of ball.

Photo 5.4
Receiving position

PERFORMANCE CUES (Contact Phase)

1. Eyes follow ball to platform.
2. Contact ball with platform slanted toward target.
3. *Do not swing arms toward target*; rather, lift "platform" with extension of legs at contact.
4. Try to keep your platform as level (parallel to thighs) as possible.
5. Contact ball just below, or at, waist level.

Photo 5.5
Contact

PERFORMANCE CUES (Follow-through Phase)

1. Platform gently moves toward target.
2. Keep hands joined throughout follow-through.
3. Eyes follow ball to target.
4. Recover quickly to join the offensive sequence.

Photo 5.6
Follow-through

LEARNING TIPS

1. Start with your body facing the server in a proper receiving position (knees bent, feet shoulder width apart or one foot slightly forward).
2. Keep hands joined, with elbows rotated inward (forming a *platform* with forearms to contact ball) throughout pass.
3. Eyes follow ball to platform; then eyes follow ball toward target.
4. Platform is slanted toward target, rather than swinging arms toward target.

5. Absorb force by guiding ball toward target with a slight extension of legs at contact.
6. Contact ball just below, or at, waist level.
7. Keep hands joined throughout follow-through.

5-3. *Self-check.* Do all the performance cues discussed in the dig preparation, contact, and follow-through phases.

5-4. *Partner-check.* Take turns demonstrating the proper dig cues as a partner checks for correct form. Repeat this 3 times with each partner.

If you experience difficulty with the readiness drills, refer to the **Performance Cues** and review each cue as presented. If you still have difficulty, ask your course instructor to assist you in applying these techniques

Common Errors and Their Correction

Error	Correction
Ball travels wildly, with arms separating.	Keep hands connected throughout contact and follow-through.
Arms follow through above shoulders.	Extension of legs, not swinging of arms, provides power. Keep arms below shoulders on follow-through.
Inconsistent trajectory off platform.	Platform needs to be flat (arms not separated) at contact. Contact ball equally with both forearms.

CRITERION TASK 5-3

Digs of Overhead Toss: Partner Checked

In a group of three, have one partner stand on the opposite side of the net and the other in the middle frontcourt (next to the net) on your side (see Illustration 5.2).

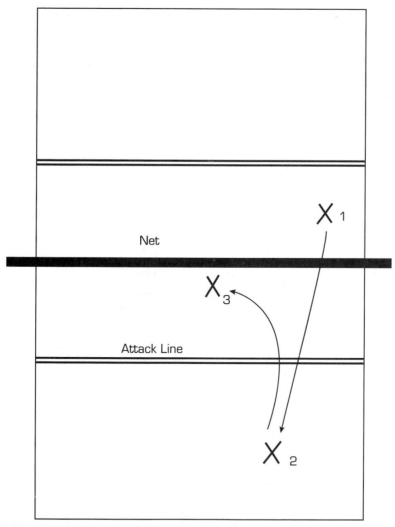

Illustration 5.2
Dig of Overhead Toss

Your first partner (1) will toss the ball over the net straight toward you (2). Gently dig the ball to your second partner (3), aiming to have the ball land within two steps of his or her position. Practice the dig in blocks of 10. Record the number of successful digs on the **Personal Recording Form**. When three individual scores reach or exceed 6 out of 10, have your partner initial and date in the space provided.

Personal Recording Form									
Block 1	Block 2	Block 3	Block 4	Block 5	Block 6	Block 7	Block 8	Block 9	Block 10
__/10	__/10	__/10	__/10	__/10	__/10	__/10	__/10	__/10	__/10

Your partner's initials _____   Date completed _____

CRITERION TASK 5-4

Digs of Overhead Spike: Partner-Checked

In a group of three, have one partner on the opposite side of the net standing on a chair or bench, and the other partner in the middle frontcourt (next to the net) on your side (see Illustration 5.3).

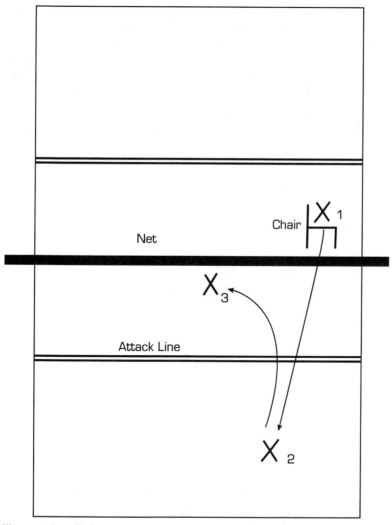

Illustration 5.3
Dig of Overhead Spike

While standing on a chair, your first partner (1) will overhand spike the ball over the net at a medium speed, straight toward you (2). Dig the ball to your second partner (3), aiming to have the ball land within two steps of his or her position. Practice the dig in blocks of 10. Record the number of successful digs on the Personal Recording Form below. When three individual scores reach or exceed 5 out of 10, have your partner initial and date in the space provided.

Personal Recording Form									
Block 1	Block 2	Block 3	Block 4	Block 5	Block 6	Block 7	Block 8	Block 9	Block 10
__/10	__/10	__/10	__/10	__/10	__/10	__/10	__/10	__/10	__/10

Your partner's initials _____   Date completed _____

CHALLENGE TASK

Combination of Serve, Bump, Set, Dink/Spike, and Block/Dig

In a group of five, with two players on one side of the net and three players on the other side of the net; serve (1), bump (2), then set (3) the ball to the frontcourt player (4), who hits the ball over the net with either a dink or spike, with player (5) attempting to block or the original server trying (1) to dig (see Illustration 5.4).

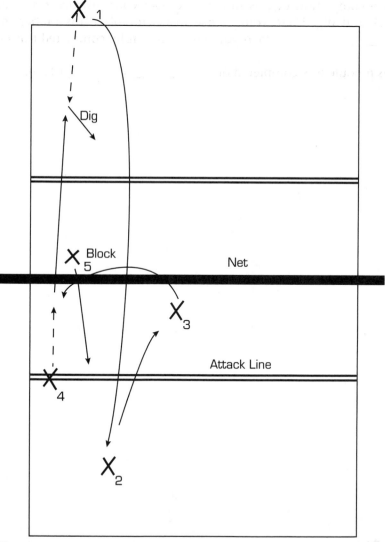

Illustration 5.4
Combination of Serve, Bump, Set, Dink/Spike, and Block/Dig

This small-group activity requires teamwork. Do this task for 15 minutes. Count how many successful five-hit combinations (serve, bump, set, dink/spike, block/dig) your team can complete.

INSTRUCTOR CHECKED

Upon completion of this module, contact your instructor to evaluate your block and dig. Have your course instructor place his or her initials here _____ when you have successfully completed this evaluation.

This module was completed on _____ (date).

MODULE **6**

PLAYING THE GAME
BASIC OFFENSIVE AND DEFENSIVE FORMATIONS

INTRODUCTION

The time has come to put all the shots together! To the uninformed observer, a game of volleyball looks like both teams are just passing the ball back and forth over the net until one team makes a mistake. In actuality, volleyball involves the use of clever and sometimes sophisticated strategies based on players' positioning on both sides of the court. Positioning is achieved by using some basic offensive and defensive formations for serving, receiving serve, offense (attacking), and defense. Learning the basic offensive and defensive formations is critical to playing the game of volleyball well, as an individual player and as a team. This volleyball knowledge module provides the bridge from working on each of the preceding skills to now applying them in gamelike situations. This requires you to work in small groups and/or in full six-person teams. Because the action in volleyball is fast and the transition from offense to defense is rapid, communication among players on your team is essential.

BASIC ROTATION PATTERN

A volleyball team of six players includes the three front-row players (closest to the net), called the left forward (LF), center forward (CF), and right forward (RF), and the three back-row players (closest to the back boundary), called the left back (LB), center back (CB), and right back (RB). Players must maintain these basic positions until the serve is hit. That is, a player cannot "overlap" another player either side to side or front to back (see Illustration 6.1). Once the serve is hit, players may move freely around the court, and the ball can be hit by any player, but not the same player twice in a row.

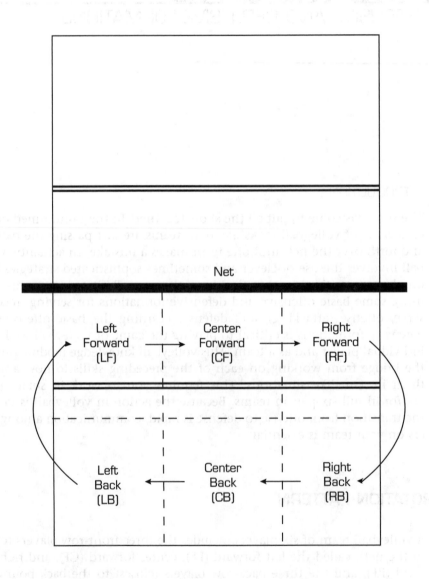

Illustration 6.1
Basic Rotation Pattern

Players on the serving team maintain their basic positions, with the RB serving, as long as they are winning points (Illustration 6.2).

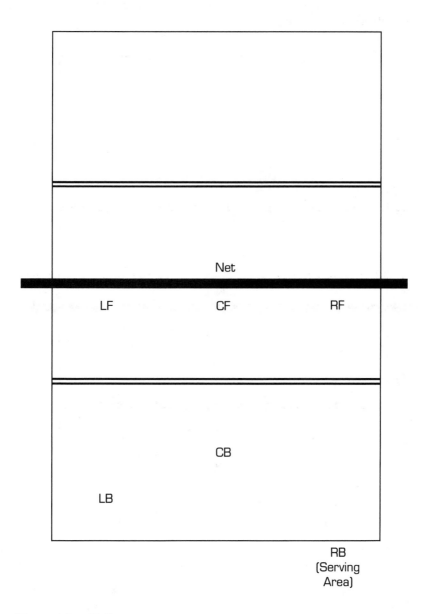

Illustration 6.2
Serving Team Positions

The basic rotation pattern (clockwise) only occurs when the nonserving team wins the rally (with no point awarded). This is referred to as a *side out* and the nonserving team rotates to become the serving team as the RF moves back to serve (see Illustration 6.3). The previous serving team will not rotate until they win their own side out.

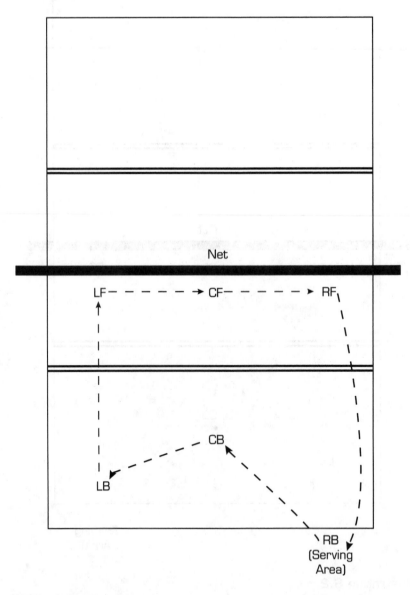

Illustration 6.3
"Side Out" Rotation with RF Rotating to Serve

For teams larger than six players, as typically found in a physical education class, substitute players wait just off the court at the net area. Once a non-serving team wins a side out, the RF moves off the court and the next substitute moves into the RB position to serve (Illustration 6.4).

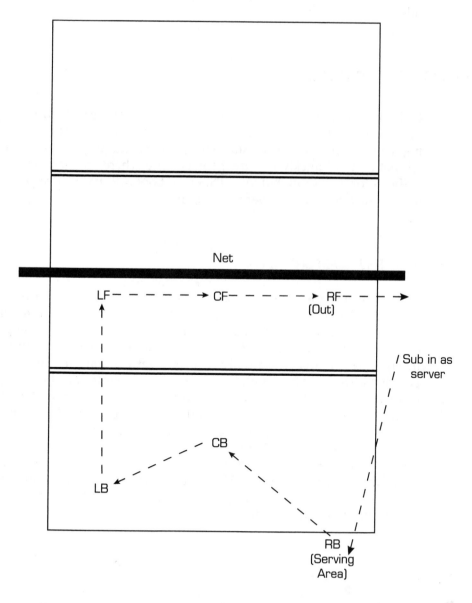

Illustration 6.4
Substitution Rotation

SCORING

Games are played to 15 points with a 2-point winning margin. A match consists of the best two out of three games or three out of five games. Points can only be scored when serving, and the same player continues to serve until a side out.

OFFENSIVE FORMATIONS

Offensive formations have two major purposes. The first is to move players into positions that take advantage of their best skills, such as setting and spiking. Once such a pattern is established, the second purpose can be to *change up* that pattern quickly to outwit the defense. There are many offensive formations for volleyball, but your PSIS workbook will familiarize you with the most basic one and some variations of it.

4–2 OFFENSIVE FORMATION

The 4–2 formation is considered the most basic offensive formation. The 4 refers to the number of attackers, and the 2 refers to the number of setters. More advanced offensive formations such as the 5–1 can be employed, but the basic 4–2 is usually sufficient for most beginning and intermediate matches. Initially, the two setters start in the CF and CB positions (though the CB player will not be the setter until rotating to the front row). This allows for a setter to always be present in the front row even after several rotations. The setter takes a position in the middle of the front row to receive the bump (underhand pass). Illustrations 6.5 through 6.7 display receiving positions for teams playing the 4–2 with the setter in the CF, LF, and RF positions, respectively. The basic receiving position is referred to as the W formation because of the alignment of the respective players. Notice in Illustrations 6.6 and 6.7 that the setter is careful not to overlap with the CF player before the incoming serve is hit.

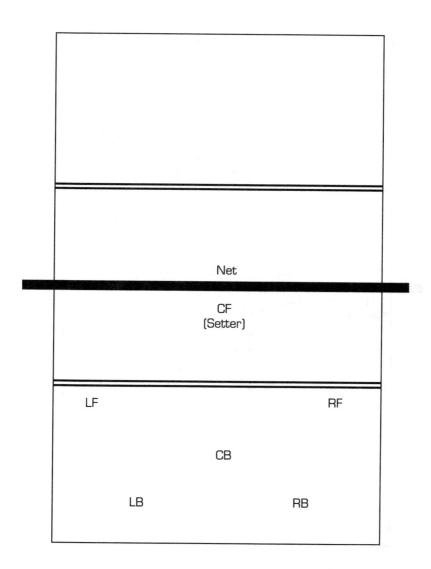

Illustration 6.5
Receiving Serve in the "W" Formation (setter in CF position)

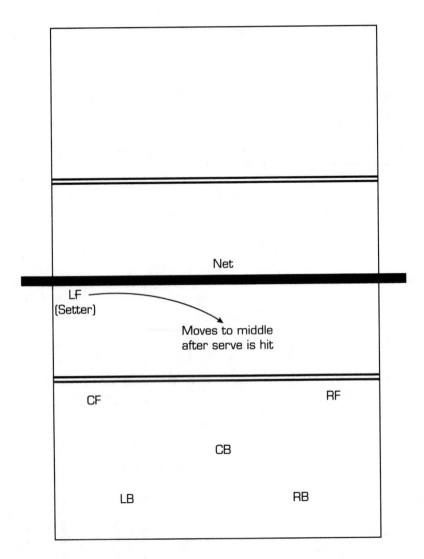

Illustration 6.6
Receiving Serve in the "W" Formation (setter in LF position)

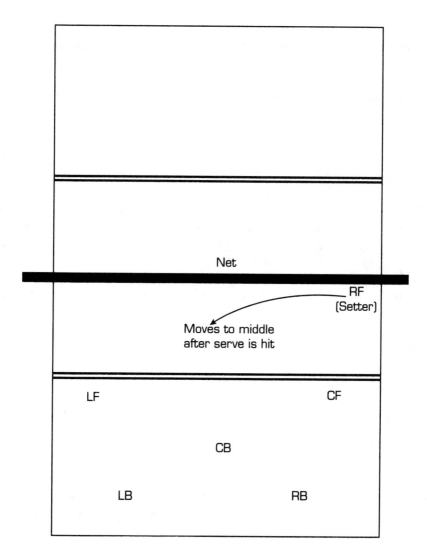

Illustration 6.7
Receiving Serve in the "W" Formation (setter in RF position)

Once the serve is hit and coming into your team's court, the setter quickly moves into the middle of the front row to receive the bump from a teammate. Setting from the middle of the front row allows for an attack (dink or spike) to be played from either sideline (by the LF and RF). Attacking from both sides makes it harder for the opposing team to position their block quickly.

LEARNING TIPS

1. Start with your body facing the server and your eyes focused on the ball.
2. Call for the ball as soon as it crosses the net toward your position.
3. Front-row players should allow any serve higher than their chest to be played by the back-row players.
4. Back-row players should allow any serve higher than their chest to go beyond the back boundary.
5. Setters should never receive the serve.

Common Errors and Their Correction

Error	Correction
Serve falls to the court between two players.	As soon as the ball crosses the net, one player must assertively call for the ball. Surrounding players turn to face the receiver, preparing for an errant bump.
Ball is bumped to setter in RF or LF position.	The setter must move quickly to the middle of the front row in order to receive the bump. Setting from the middle allows for an attack from either sideline (making for a more difficult block).
Setter receives serve.	The setter should take a position close to the net in order to watch for the upcoming bump.

READINESS DRILL

6-1.   Join a team of six players and go to one side of the net. Each player will assume one of the six positions. Refer back to Illustration 6.1 if you need a reminder. Have a seventh student stand on the sideline and call out each of the situations listed below, pause for 10 seconds, and then say "Go" to the players on the court. At the signal, each member of the team should move to the correct spot on the court for his or her position. Once in position, the student on the sideline compares the team's positions to those shown in Illustrations 6.1 through 6.7.

1.	Basic rotation pattern	Illustration 6.1
2.	Serving positions	Illustration 6.2
3.	Side out rotation, RF to serve	Illustration 6.3
4.	Substitution rotation	Illustration 6.4
5.	W for receiving serve, CF setter	Illustration 6.5
6.	W for receiving serve, LF setter	Illustration 6.6
7.	W for receiving serve, RF setter	Illustration 6.7

Randomly repeat this set of formations 3 times, with each player taking three different positions at the start.

DEFENSIVE FORMATIONS

Just as the team on offense tries to move its players into their most effective positions, the defense can also use strategic formations to prepare for the expected shot to its court by the offense. Again, there are many different defensive formations, but your PSIS course will familiarize you with the most basic one, allowing you and your team to mount an effective defense at the beginning level of play.

2-1-3 DEFENSIVE FORMATION

The 2-1-3 formation is considered the most basic defensive formation. The 2 refers to the number of blockers , the 1 refers to the player positioned behind the blockers, and the 3 refers to number of backcourt players. Similar to the

4–2 offense, other advanced defensive formations can be employed, but the basic 2–1–3 is usually sufficient for most beginning and intermediate matches. Initially, the base defensive formation is similar to the W receiving serve formation, except the LF and RF are placed at the net in preparation to block (see Illustration 6.8).

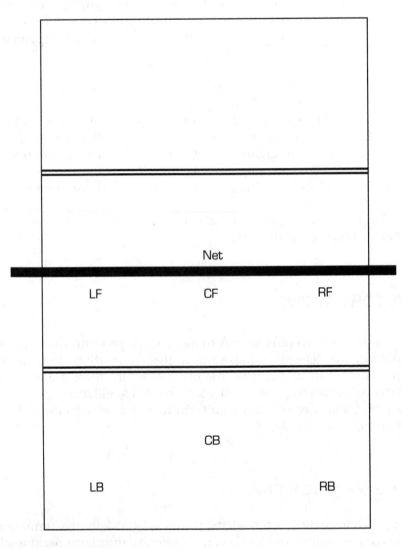

Illustration 6.8
Base Defensive Formation

As soon as the opposing team's setter passes the ball toward the attacking sideline, the two front row blockers quickly slide across in front of the attacker. For example (Illustration 6.9), if the attack is coming from the opposing LF, the CF and RF take a blocking position in front of the attacker, the CB slides across to cover the dink over the outstretched hands of the blockers, and the LF, LB, and RB take positions in an arc covering crosscourt and down-the-line spikes.

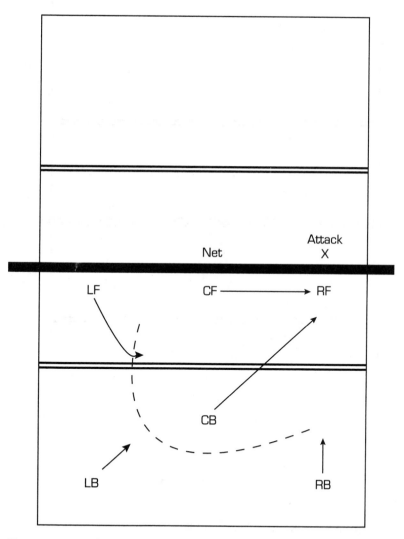

Illustration 6.9
Covering an Attack from the Opposing LF

If the attack is coming from the opposing RF (Illustration 6.10), the CF and LF take a blocking position in front of the attacker, the CB slides across to cover the dink over the outstretched hands of the blockers, and the RF, LB, and RB take positions in an arc covering crosscourt and down-the-line spikes.

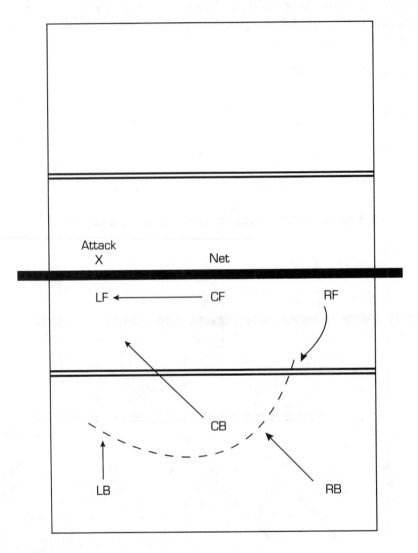

Illustration 6.10
Covering an Attack from the Opposing RF

LEARNING TIPS

1. Start with your body facing the opposing team and your eyes focused on the ball.
2. Call out the side of the attack as soon as the setter places the ball upward.
3. Front-row players must be ready to slide across to block or be prepared for a deflected ball from their teammates.
4. Back-row players must be ready to move forward to cover dinks or be prepared to dig a hard spike into the open court.
5. A deflected ball (partially blocked) or free ball (passed across by the opposing team with little force) must be called for as quickly as possible to setup your counterattack.

Common Errors and Their Correction

Error	Correction
Dink falls to the floor over outstretched hands of blockers.	CB must quickly slide forward to cover dink.
Ball travels between blockers.	CF must quickly slide across to block from a position side by side with the LF or RF.
Ball deflects off block and falls to floor.	All teammates must be ready for an errant deflection off the block and be prepared to quickly move toward ball to keep it in play.

READINESS DRILL

6-2. Join a team of six players and go to one side of the net. Each player will assume one of the six positions. Refer back to Illustration 6.1 if you need a reminder. Have a seventh student stand on the sideline and call out each of the situations listed below, pause for 10 seconds, and then say "Go" to the players on the court. At the signal, each member of the team should move to the correct spot on the court for his or her position. Once in position, the student on the sideline compares the team's positioning to those shown in Illustrations 6.8 through 6.10.

1.	Basic defensive formation	Illustration 6.8
2.	Attack from opposing LF	Illustration 6.9
3.	Attack from opposing RF	Illustration 6.10

Randomly repeat this set of formations 3 times, with each player taking three different positions at the start.

MODULE 7

VOLLEYBALL KNOWLEDGE FOR BEGINNERS

INTRODUCTION

This final unit consists of the volleyball knowledge needed to ensure that you know enough about the rules and strategies of volleyball to begin playing. Access to official volleyball rules is as easy as checking your school library or contacting USA Volleyball at http://www.volleyball.org/pub/rule_book.htm. Or you can write them at the following address:

> USA Volleyball
> 1 Olympic Plaza
> Colorado Springs, CO 80909-1740.

Instead of listing every rule, this unit briefly summarizes key rules to get you playing as quickly as possible.

BASIC VOLLEYBALL RULES AND TERMINOLOGY

In basic terms, the object of volleyball is to hit the ball across the net in such a manner that your opponents cannot return it. Teachers and coaches instruct their students and athletes to use a three-hit combination of bump, set, and spike, if possible. The rules do not, however, mandate that a three-hit combination must be used. Indeed, it is perfectly legal to return your opponent's serve with a bump completely across the net. Your team misses out, of course, on any opportunity to counterattack.

COIN FLIP

A match begins with a coin flip to determine which team serves first and on which side of the court each team will start. The captain winning the coin flip has the choice of serving first, choosing a side, or forcing the other captain to choose first.

OVERLAPPING

All players must be in their proper positions prior to the serve. That is, the front row players must be in front of the back row players, and the CF must be between the LF and RF; and the CB must be between the LB and RB. Once the serve is contacted, players may move freely around the court. Improper overlapping results in a side out or loss of point.

SERVICE

The RB has 5 seconds to serve the ball from within the serving area (an area 9 feet 10 inches from the sideline). The serve must be hit with one hand (either open or closed) and cross the net without touching. Only one fault is allowed in volleyball. The server may not step on the back boundary line or step into the court until after contacting the ball. The same player continues to serve until the serving team loses the rally, resulting in a side out for the nonserving team.

THREE HITS

Teams must send the ball back across the net within a maximum of three hits. If the first touch is a block, however, the blocking team still gets their full three hits. A double hit occurs when a single player contacts the ball more than once without a teammate contacting it between the successive contacts, which is not allowed. If the first touch is a block, however, the blocking player may contact the ball again. The ball may contact any part of the body above, and including, the waist.

CARRY OR HELD BALL

If the ball momentarily comes to rest in the hands (or fingers) of a player, the ball is considered held. A carry often occurs when a player attempts to set a poor bump. This results in a side out or loss of point.

HANDS OVER NET

Blockers are allowed to place their hands over the net to block the ball. They must, however, not touch the net and may only deflect a ball that has been struck with the intent of clearing the net; that is, they cannot reach across and spike the ball down. Only front-row players are allowed to reach over the net.

BALL ON NET

The ball is still in play when hitting the net. Players may deflect a ball hit into the net back across the net (providing this occurs within three hits). Players are not allowed to touch the net with any part of their body. As long as it does not interfere with the opponent, a player may step under the net with one foot when landing or chasing a free ball.

ATTACK LINE

Only front-row players are allowed to spike in front of the attack line. Back-row players may spike as long as they initially jump from behind the attack line.

SIDE AND BACK BOUNDARIES

Players may chase a ball beyond the boundaries. The ball must, however, travel across the net between the two outside poles. A ball perceived to be flying beyond the boundaries must be allowed to land before being caught by a player. A ball landing on the side or back boundary is considered in play.

VOLLEYBALL KNOWLEDGE QUIZ

Name _____ Date _____

1. When hitting an underhand serve, you should to contact the ball at approximately:
    - A.   Chest level
    - B.   Knee level
    - C.   Waist level
    - D.   Shoulderlevel

2. An underhand serve that travels high but not far enough to cross the net probably results from the following error:
    - A.   Hand contacts back rather than bottom of ball.
    - B.   Hand contact bottom rather than back of ball.
    - C.   Ball is contacted with a closed hand.
    - D.   Ball is spinning at contact.

3. To achieve power with the overhead serve, you should:
    - A.   Step forward with opposite foot of hitting hand.
    - B.   Step forward with same foot of hitting hand.
    - C.   Toss ball over nonhitting shoulder.
    - D.   Keep feet stationary.

4. An overhead serve that travels hard but not high enough to cross the net probably results from the following error:
    - A.   Ball is spinning at contact.
    - B.   Hand contacts back rather than bottom of ball.
    - C.   Hand contact botto, rather than back of ball.
    - D.   Ball is tossed over non-hitting shoulder.

5. The bump is executed by contacting the ball at approximately:

    A.   Knee level

    B.   Chest level

    C.   Shoulder level

    D.   Waist level

6. Erratic bumps often result because:

    A.   The platform is flat at contact.

    B.   The legs extend at contact.

    C.   The arms follow through above shoulders.

    D.   The knees are bent at contact.

7. The set is executed by thinking of:

    A.   Contacting the ball with a flat platform.

    B.   Contacting the ball by looking through a window.

    C.   Contacting the ball with the palms of your hands.

    D.   Contacting the ball at shoulder level.

8. Slapping the ball when setting is probably a result of the following error:

    A.   Contacting the ball with a flat platform.

    B.   Contacting the ball by looking through a window.

    C.   Contacting the ball with the palms of your hands.

    D.   Contacting the ball at shoulder level.

9. To forcibly spike the ball, contact the ball:

    A.   With your fingers extended.

    B.   With your chest facing the target.

    C.   With your knees bent.

    D.   With your arm fully extended.

10. To dink the ball effectively, contact the ball:

    A.   With your fingertips.

    B.   With your chest facing the target.

    C.   With your knees bent.

    D.   With your arm bent to absorb the force.

11. When blocking, time your jump so that:

    A.   You jump at the same time as your opponent.

    B.   You jump just before your opponent.

    C.   You jump just after your opponent.

    D.   You jump with one hand extended completely.

12. A block traveling between two blockers is probably the result of the following error:

    A.   Blockers are too far apart.

    B.   Blockers did not cover the crosscourt spike.

    C.   Blockers jumped too high.

    D.   Blockers hands are facing downward.

13. Digging a hard spike is similar to:

    A.   Overhead passing.

    B.   Overhead setting.

    C.   Underhand setting.

    D.   Underhand passing.

14. In the 4–2 offensive formation, who do you not want to receive the serve?

    A.   RF

    B.   RB

    C.   LF

    D.   Setter

15. In the 4-2 offensive formation, the receiving serve position is called:

      A. The U formation.

      B. The W formation.

      C. The X formation.

      D. The base formation.

16. Back-row players are not allowed to:

      A. Spike from behind the attack line.

      B. Spike from in front of the attack line.

      C. Set from the back row.

      D. Receive serve in front of the attack line.

17. To guarantee not to overlap, the setter in the RF position must stand:

      A. In front of the CF.

      B. To the right of the CF.

      C. Behind the CF.

      D. To the left of the CF.

18. In the 2–1–3 defensive formation, who typically covers the dink over the block?

      A. Setter

      B. RB

      C. LB

      D. CB

19. How many blockers are there in the 2–1–3 defensive formation?

      A. 2

      B. 1

      C. 3

      D. 4

20. A free ball results when:

    A. The opposing team spikes the ball over your block.

    B. The opposing team passes the ball across with little force.

    C. Your team forgets to call for the ball.

    D. Your server hits the top of the net.

Personal Progress Chart for PSIS Volleyball

Module		1	2	3	4	5	6	7	8	9	10	11	12	13	14	15
7	Volleyball Knowledge Quiz															
6	Basic Offinsive and Defensive Patterns															
5	Blocking and Digging															
4	Dinking and Spiking															
3	Underhand and Overhead Passing															
2	Underhand and Overhead Serves															
1	Stretching															
	Weeks in Class	1	2	3	4	5	6	7	8	9	10	11	12	13	14	15